DATE DUE

Celebrating the Peoples and Civilizations of Southeast Asia™

THE PEOPLE OF
LAOS

Dolly Brittan

The Rosen Publishing Group's
PowerKids Press™
New York

Published in 1997 by The Rosen Publishing Group, Inc.
29 East 21st Street, New York, NY 10010

First Edition

Book Design: Danielle Primiceri

Photo Credits: Cover © Nevada Wier/Image Bank (background), © Mark Downey/Viesti Associates, Inc.; pp. 4, 12 (bottom inset) © Nevada Wier/Image Bank; pp. 7, 8, 11, 12 (background and middle inset), 16, 20 © Joe Viesti/Viesti Associates, Inc.; pp. 12, 15 (top inset) © Viesti Associates, Inc.; p. 19 © Archive Photos.

Brittan, Dolly.
  The people of Laos / Dolly Brittan.
      p.   cm. (Celebrating the peoples and civilizations of Southeast Asia)
  Summary: Examines the history, language, ethnicities, religion, food, and economy of Laos.
  ISBN 0-8239-5124-3
  1. Laos—Juvenile literature. [1. Laos.] I. Title. II. Series.
  DS555.3.B75 1997
  915.94—dc21   97-5879
                                                                    CIP
                                                                    AC

Manufactured in the United States of America

Contents

CHINA

VIETNAM

MYANMAR

LAOS

Vientiane

THAILAND

South China
Sea

CAMBODIA

A Country Called Laos

Laos (LAH-ohs) is a country in Southeast Asia. It is surrounded by China, Vietnam, Thailand, and Myanmar. Laos was formed nearly 700 years ago. Groups of people from Thailand moved south. They began their own country. It was called Lan Xang, which means "Kingdom of a Million Elephants." Over the years, Lan Xang ruled over many other countries. But in the 1700s, it split into two countries. In the early 1900s, it became one country again and was called Laos, but was under the rule of France. Laos became **independent** (in-dee-PEN-dent) once again in 1975.

Laos has a long history. But the natural beauty of the land has stayed largely untouched through the years.

The Capital

The capital of Laos is **Vientiane** (VIN-tee-ahn). Vientiane is also called the "City of Sandalwood." **Fragrant** (FRAY-grent) sandalwood trees are scattered throughout the city. Vientiane overlooks the Mekong River, which runs through most of Laos.

Much of Laos is covered with mountains and forests. It is hard to build roads there. There are no railroads and few highways. In many ways, Laos has looked the same for hundreds of years.

*Vientiane is the capital of Laos.
It is also the largest city in Laos.* ▶

Living in Laos

Four million people live in Laos. About half of those people belong to a group called the Lao. Other groups of people include the Lao Theung, or "Mountain People," the Hmong, and the Yao. There are also many Vietnamese, Chinese, and Indian people who live in Laos.

Many **Laotians** (lah-OH-shunz), or people who live in Laos, are farmers. They grow crops such as rice, coffee, tobacco, sugarcane, and cotton. Many farmers sell their goods at the local market.

Markets like this one are set up in many cities and villages in Laos.

The Language

The people of Laos speak the language Lao. Lao is a **tonal** (TOW-nul) language. That means that the same word can mean different things if you change the tone you use to say the word. There are six tones in Lao.

Some Laotians also speak other languages, such as Thai, French, and Hmong. Children also learn to speak, read, and write English in school.

Although there are several languages spoken in Laos, most people speak Lao. ▶

Religion and Culture

Many Laotians follow a religion called **Buddhism** (BOO-dizm). Buddhists follow the teachings of a man called the Buddha. Buddha means "the **enlightened** (en-LY-tend) one." Enlightenment is the complete understanding of life and of your place in life. There are many Buddhist *wats*, or **temples** (TEM-pulz), in Laos.

Other Laotians are **animists** (AN-ih-mists). Animists believe in **respecting** (ree-SPEK-ting) all living things.

Religion plays a large role in the lives of many Laotians.
◀ *There are many temples and statues of the Buddha throughout the country.*

Morning Market

Many Laotians shop at markets rather than stores. A market is set up in cities, such as Vientiane, every morning. Women carry fruits and vegetables to the market in large baskets. They set up their stands under bright, colorful umbrellas. Other women sell slippery eels, tin buckets, woven baskets, pottery, Laotian silk, and **sinh** (SIN), which is handwoven cloth.

Girls and women wear skirts made from *sinh* and Western-style shirts. Boys and men usually wear shirts and pants. Nearly everyone wears sandals.

Women bring their goods to the market to sell. ▶

Food

Laotian food is often hot and spicy. It is eaten with sticky rice. One Laotian dish is called *orlam*. It is made with pork, buffalo skin, mushrooms, and eggplant. Most Laotian dishes are flavored with herbs such as lemongrass and sandalwood.

Because there are so many people from other countries who live in Laos, the foods from those countries are eaten there too.

◀ *Laotians cook special dishes for celebrations.*

Working Elephants

The forests are home to many animals, such as tigers, leopards, and elephants. The Laotians have found a way for the elephants to help them move things through the forest.

Many kinds of trees grow in the forests of Laos, including the teak tree. The strong wood from the teak tree is used to build ships, furniture, and many other things.

Men cut down teak trees. Then they use elephants to drag the **lumber** (LUM-ber) from the forests. It is easier for elephants than for trucks to get through the thick forests.

In Laos, elephants are trained to go into the thick forests and pull out the lumber. ▶

Getting Around in Laos

Most Laotians use the Mekong River to travel long distances or move goods from one place to another. Although there are no railroads, there are many small roads or trails. In larger towns, small vans have been made into open-backed buses.

Many people take **samlors** (SAM-lorz), or bicycle taxis, to get around cities such as Vientiane. Other people use motorbike taxis. Still others drive cars.

Laotians have many ways of traveling from place to place, including using bicycles and open-backed buses.

Laotians Today

The natural beauty of Laos has stayed largely untouched through the years. Many Laotians still grow their own food. Laotians believe in being polite and respecting others. Many of their **customs** (KUS-tumz) come from their religion. Many Laotians do not have the things that people in other countries are used to, such as televisions or computers. But they have the **security** (seh-KYUR-ih-tee) and peace of living as their ancestors did.

Glossary

animist (AN-ih-mist) A person who believes in the religion of animism, in which people are taught to respect all living things.

Buddhism (BOO-dizm) A religion based on the teachings of the Buddha.

custom (KUS-tum) A cultural tradition that is passed down from parent to child.

enlightened (en-LY-tend) Having an understanding of yourself and the world around you.

fragrant (FRAY-grent) Having a good smell.

independent (in-dee-PEN-dent) To think and act for yourself.

Laos (LAH-ohs) A country in Southeast Asia.

Laotian (lah-OH-shun) A person who was born in or lives in Laos.

lumber (LUM-ber) Wood from trees.

respect (ree-SPEKT) To honor.

samlor (SAM-lor) A traditional Laotian dish.

security (seh-KYUR-ih-tee) Feeling safe and free from danger.

sinh (SIN) Traditional handwoven cloth made in Laos.

temple (TEM-pul) A place of worship.

tonal (TOW-nul) Having to do with the tone or sound of something.

Vientiane (VIN-tee-ahn) The capital city of Laos.

Index

11-10-04